Congressional
Research Service
Informing the legislative debate since 1914 _____

Statutory Authority for the Chemical Facility Anti-Terrorism Standards (CFATS): A Comparison of H.R. 4007 and P.L. 109-295, Section 550

Dana A. Shea
Specialist in Science and Technology Policy

July 17, 2014

Congressional Research Service

7-5700

www.crs.gov

R43650

Summary

The 109th Congress provided the Department of Homeland Security (DHS) with statutory authority to regulate chemical facilities for security purposes through Section 550 of the Department of Homeland Security Appropriations Act, 2007 (P.L. 109-295). This statutory authority contains a termination date, after which the statutory authority expires. The current termination date is October 4, 2014.

Subsequent Congresses have attempted to provide a new authorization for the current statutory authority, which DHS implements through the Chemical Facility Anti-Terrorism Standards (CFATS). In the 113th Congress, several bills have been introduced in the House of Representatives and the Senate. One, H.R. 4007, has passed the House.

H.R. 4007, as passed by the House, incorporates much of the language in the existing statute. Consequently, its authorities would generally encompass the existing authorities, and its implementation by DHS may retain a similar regulatory structure. Indeed, the bill expressly would allow DHS to use existing CFATS regulations to implement its provisions.

Unlike the existing statute, H.R. 4007, as passed by the House, would amend the Homeland Security Act of 2002 (P.L. 107-296, as amended). It would create a new title, Title XXI, called Chemical Facility Anti-Terrorism Standards. Another key difference between H.R. 4007, as passed by the House, and the existing statute is the absence of a termination date for the statutory authority. The statutory authority would be permanent, though H.R. 4007, as passed by the House, includes a limited three-year authorization of appropriations.

Other provisions in H.R. 4007, as passed by the House, would add to the Secretary's responsibilities. For example, H.R. 4007, as passed by the House, would require certain outreach to chemical facilities, assistance to regulated small chemical facilities, and reporting by DHS and the Government Accountability Office (GAO) on program performance.

Finally, H.R. 4007, as passed by the House, would modify the discretion of the Secretary of Homeland Security in various areas. The Secretary's existing discretion to establish criteria for risk-based performance standards would be maintained. H.R. 4007, as passed by the House, would limit the Secretary's discretion when it expressly requires DHS to accept alternative security programs with respect to site security plans, mandate specific approaches with respect to personnel surety, and restrict the Secretary's ability to require covered chemical facilities to submit information to DHS about personnel entering the facility. H.R. 4007, as passed by the House, would expand the discretion of the Secretary by no longer limiting application of the statutory authority to high-risk facilities. Some experts might argue that modifying the Secretary's discretion might lead to a less efficient regulatory program. Other experts might argue that the Secretary's discretion might need further modification in order to reflect congressional intent.

Contents

S tate and federal governments have long regulated safety practices at chemical facilities because of the potential harm that a large, sudden release of hazardous chemicals could cause to nearby people. Even before the terrorist attacks of 2001, congressional policy makers expressed concern about the security vulnerabilities of these facilities, which historically engaged in security activities on a voluntary basis. After the 2001 attacks and the decision by several states to begin regulating security at chemical facilities, Congress again considered requiring federal security regulations to mitigate risks.

In 2006, the 109th Congress passed legislation providing the Department of Homeland Security (DHS) with statutory authority to regulate chemical facilities for security purposes.[1] The statute explicitly identified some DHS authorities and left other aspects to the discretion of the Secretary of Homeland Security. The Secretary exercised that discretion when implementing this authority through regulations called the Chemical Facility Anti-Terrorism Standards (CFATS). The statute contains a "sunset provision" that causes the statutory authority to expire. Subsequent Congresses have extended the termination date of this authority to October 4, 2014.[2] Advocacy groups, industry stakeholders, and policy makers have called for Congress to reauthorize this authority, though they disagree about the preferred approach. Members of Congress have introduced bills taking several different approaches to the issue of reauthorization in the current and previous Congresses. Congress may extend the existing authority, revise the existing authority to resolve potentially contentious issues, or allow the authority to lapse.

In the 113th Congress, Members have introduced several proposals in the House and the Senate that would extend the statutory termination date, modify the underlying statutory authority, or both.[3] The House of Representatives passed H.R. 4007, the Chemical Facility Anti-Terrorism Standards Program Authorization and Accountability Act of 2014, on July 8, 2014.[4] The House Committee on Homeland Security had amended the bill as forwarded by its Subcommittee on Cybersecurity, Infrastructure Protection, and Security Technologies and reported it to the House of Representatives with a favorable recommendation, as amended.[5]

This report compares H.R. 4007, as passed by the House, to the existing statutory authority. It provides a brief overview of H.R. 4007, as passed by the House; identifies select differences for comparison; analyzes each section of H.R. 4007, as passed by the House, in the context of the existing statutory authority; and discusses several policy issues raised by the Obama Administration in the context of chemical facility security legislation.

---

[1] Section 550, P.L. 109-295, Department of Homeland Security Appropriations Act, 2007.

[2] The original statutory authority expired on October 4, 2009, three years after enactment. Congress has incrementally extended this authority through multiple appropriation acts and continuing resolutions. Most recently, the Consolidated Appropriations Act, 2014 (P.L. 113-76) extended the statutory authority through October 4, 2014.

[3] For more information about the policy debates surrounding DHS regulation of chemical facility security, see CRS Report R42918, *Chemical Facility Security: Issues and Options for the 113th Congress*, by Dana A. Shea.

[4] The bill has been referred in the Senate to the Senate Committee on Homeland Security and Governmental Affairs.

[5] H.Rept. 113-491. The House Committee on Homeland Security considered the bill and ordered it to be reported as amended on April 30, 2014.

Overview of H.R. 4007, as Passed by the House

H.R. 4007 has both similarities and differences with the existing statute. H.R. 4007, as passed by the House, incorporates much of the language in the existing statutory authority. Consequently, its authorities would generally encompass the existing authorities, and its implementation by DHS may retain a similar regulatory structure. Indeed, the bill expressly would allow DHS to use existing CFATS regulations to implement its provisions.

In contrast with the existing statute, H.R. 4007, as passed by the House, would amend the Homeland Security Act of 2002 (P.L. 107-296, as amended). It would create a new title, Title XXI, called Chemical Facility Anti-Terrorism Standards. Another key difference between H.R. 4007, as passed by the House, and the existing statute is the absence of a statutory termination date. The statutory authority would be permanent, though H.R. 4007, as passed by the House, explicitly authorizes appropriations for three years.

H.R. 4007, as passed by the House, contains additional legislative language that would add to the Secretary's responsibilities. For example, H.R. 4007, as passed by the House, would require certain outreach to chemical facilities, assistance to regulated small chemical facilities, and reporting by DHS and the Government Accountability Office (GAO) on program performance.

Finally, H.R. 4007, as passed by the House, would modify the discretion of the Secretary of Homeland Security in various areas. The Secretary's existing discretion to establish criteria for risk-based performance standards would be maintained. H.R. 4007, as passed by the House, would limit the Secretary's discretion when it expressly requires DHS to accept alternative security programs with respect to site security plans, mandate specific approaches with respect to personnel surety, and restrict the Secretary's ability to require covered chemical facilities to submit information to DHS about personnel at the facility. Finally, H.R. 4007, as passed by the House, would expand the discretion of the Secretary by no longer limiting application of the statutory authority to high-risk facilities. Some experts might argue that modifying the Secretary's discretion might lead to a less efficient regulatory program. Other experts might argue that the Secretary's discretion might need further modification in order to reflect congressional intent.

Table 1 below highlights selected differences between H.R. 4007, as passed by the House, and P.L. 109-295, Section 550, as amended. For a fuller comparison of legislative text, see **Table A-1** in the **Appendix**.

Table 1. Selected Differences between H.R. 4007, as Passed by the House, and P.L. 109-295, Section 550, as Amended

Topic	H.R. 4007, as Passed by the House	P.L. 109-295, Section 550, as Amended
Risk-based performance standards	Secretary shall establish risk-based performance standards designed to protect covered chemical facilities and chemical facilities of interest from acts of terrorism and other security risk [Sec. 2(a) "Sec. 2101(a)"]	Secretary shall issue interim final regulations establishing risk-based performance standards for security of chemical facilities [Sec. 550(a)]

Topic	H.R. 4007, as Passed by the House	P.L. 109-295, Section 550, as Amended
Facility vulnerability assessment	Covered chemical facilities and chemical facilities of interest must submit security vulnerability assessments [Sec. 2(a) "Sec. 2101(a)"]	Facilities presenting high levels of security risk must submit security vulnerability assessments [Sec. 550(a)]
Site security plans	Covered chemical facilities and chemical facilities of interest must develop and implement site security plans [Sec. 2(a) "Sec. 2101(a)"]	Facilities presenting high levels of security risk must develop and implement site security plans [Sec. 550(a)]
Facility use of alternative security programs	Facilities may use alternative security programs reviewed and approved by the Secretary to meet the site security requirement [Sec. 2(a) "Sec. 2101(c)(2)"]	No comparable provision
Consultation with GAO	Secretary may consult with GAO to investigate the feasibility and applicability of a third-party accreditation program [Sec. 2(a) "Sec. 2101(c)(4)"]	No comparable provision
Third-party personnel use and training	Authorized as auditors and inspectors with certain requirements [Sec. 2(a) "Sec. 2101(d)(1)"]	No comparable provision
Training of departmental inspectors	Secretary required to prescribe certain standards for training and retraining [Sec. 2(a) "Sec. 2101(d)(1)(D)"]	No comparable provision
Personnel surety program	Program shall not require multiple submissions of information, shall provide feedback to facilities, and shall provide certain types of redress for individuals [Sec. 2(a) "Sec. 2101(d)(3)(A)"]	No comparable provision
Personnel surety implementation	Facilities may meet personnel surety requirements by using any federal screening program that periodically vets individuals against the terrorist screening database [Sec. 2(a) "Sec. 2101(d)(3)(B)"]	No comparable provision
Development of common personnel surety credential	Directs Security Screening Coordination Office to expedite credential development [Sec. 2(a) "Sec. 2101(d)(3)(C)"]	No comparable provision
Facility access	Prohibits the Secretary from requiring a facility to submit information about individuals unless vetted by DHS or identified as a terrorism security risk [Sec. 2(a) "Sec. 2101(d)(4)"]	No comparable provision
Identification of chemical facilities of interest	Requires consultation with other federal agencies, states, and relevant business associations [Sec. 2(a) "Sec. 2101(e)(1)"]	No comparable provision
Risk assessment	Requires development of risk assessment approach and tiering methodology [Sec. 2(a) "Sec. 2101(e)(2)(A)"]	No comparable provision
Criteria for determining security risk	Shall include relevant threat information, potential consequences, and facility vulnerability [Sec. 2(a) "Sec. 2101(e)(2)(B)"]	No comparable provision
Records of tiering changes	Secretary shall maintain records regarding changes in tiering leading to a determination that a facility is no longer regulated [Sec. 2(a) "Sec. 2101(e)(3)"]	No comparable provision

Topic	H.R. 4007, as Passed by the House	P.L. 109-295, Section 550, as Amended
Definition of covered chemical facility	Chemical facility of interest that, based on review of certain information, meets certain risk criteria specified in the bill [Sec. 2(a) "Sec. 2101(f)(1)"]	Chemical facilities that the Secretary determines present high levels of security risk [Sec. 550(a)]
Definition of chemical facility of interest	Facility holding a chemical of interest designated under 6 CFR Appendix A[a] at a threshold quantity that meets relevant risk-related criteria specified in the bill [Sec. 2(a) "Sec. 2101(f)(2)"]	No comparable provision
Sharing of information with first responders	Through state, local, and regional fusion centers via the Homeland Security Information Network and the Homeland Secure Data Network [Sec. 2(a) "Sec. 2102(c)"]	No comparable provision
Whistleblower protections	Secretary shall publish on the DHS website and in other materials made available to the public the whistleblower protections that an individual providing such information would have [Sec. 2(a) "Sec. 2104"]	No comparable provision
Eliminating duplicative provisions	Secretary authorized to eliminate provisions of law that are duplicative between CFATS and the Transportation Security Administration rail transportation security rule[b] [Sec. 2(a) "Sec. 2105(c)(1)"]	No comparable provision
Exemption for rail facilities	Cargo or passenger rail facilities are exempt from CFATS if subject to rail cargo transportation security regulation [Sec. 2(a) "Sec. 2105(c)(2)"]	No comparable provision
Departmental report to Congress	Report certifying progress in identifying chemical facilities of interest, certifying the development of a risk assessment approach and tiering methodology, and assessing implementation of certain recommendations [Sec. 2(a) "Sec. 2106(a)"]	No comparable provision
GAO report	Semiannual reports on the implementation of the act for two years [Sec. 2(a) "Sec. 2106(b)"]	No comparable provision
Exclusive authority	Secretary shall rely exclusively on authorities provided to identify chemicals of interest, designate chemicals of interest, and determine facility security risk [Sec. 2(a) "Sec. 2107(d)"]	No comparable provision
Small covered chemical facilities	Secretary may provide guidance and other assistance regarding physical security to covered chemical facilities employing fewer than 350 employees that are not branches or subsidiaries of another company [Sec. 2(a) "Sec. 2108"]	No comparable provision
Outreach to chemical facilities of interest	Secretary shall coordinate with heads of other federal and state agencies and relevant business associations to make certain information available [Sec. 2(a) "Sec. 2108"]	No comparable provision
Authorization of appropriations	$87,436,000 annually for fiscal years 2015, 2016, and 2017 [Sec. 2(a) "Sec. 2110"]	No comparable provision
Third-party assessment	Third-party assessment of terrorism vulnerabilities associated with current implementation of CFATS [Sec. 2(c)]	No comparable provision
Performance reporting	Secretary shall submit a plan for the use of metrics and incorporation of metrics into program [Sec. 2(d)]	No comparable provision
Termination date	No comparable provision	Authority terminates on October 4, 2014 [Sec. 550(b)]

Source: CRS analysis of H.R. 4007, as passed by the House, and P.L. 109-295, Section 550, as amended.

Notes: This table identifies selected differences. For a fuller comparison of legislative text, see **Table A-1** in the **Appendix**.

a. This likely is a reference to 6 CFR 27 Appendix A, which contains the list of chemicals of interest currently used under CFATS.

b. The bill language cites "Subpart 3." This likely is a reference to Subpart B, which contains the rail transportation security rule.

Section by Section Discussion

This section of the report discusses each section of H.R. 4007, as passed by the House, and provides policy analysis regarding selected provisions in the context of the existing statutory authority and CFATS regulation. For a direct comparison of the bill language and the existing statutory authority, see **Table A-1**. H.R. 4007, as passed by the House, contains three sections.

Section 1, Short Title

Section 1 of H.R. 4007, as passed by the House, contains the act's short title. The existing authority has no comparable provision.

Section 2, Chemical Facility Anti-Terrorism Standards Program

Section 2 of H.R. 4007, as passed by the House, consists of amendments to the Homeland Security Act of 2002 and contains four subsections. **Subsection 2(a)** would create a new title, Title XXI, called Chemical Facility Anti-Terrorism Standards, in the Homeland Security Act. This new title would have ten sections as described below.

Section 2101, Chemical Facility Anti-Terrorism Standards Program

Section 2101 of the new title has six subsections that are analyzed below.

Establishment of Risk-Based Performance Standards

Subsection 2101(a) of the new title would establish a Chemical Facility Anti-Terrorism Standards Program and direct the Secretary to establish risk-based performance standards under that program. These standards would be designed to protect chemical facilities that the Secretary determines are either a "covered chemical facility" or a "chemical facility of interest" from acts of terrorism and other security risks. Later provisions would define a "chemical facility of interest" as a facility that holds certain chemicals above a certain quantity as determined by the Secretary and a "covered chemical facility" as a chemical facility of interest that the Secretary determines meets certain security risk criteria. This subsection would also require both chemical facilities of interest and covered chemical facilities to submit security vulnerability assessments and develop and implement site security plans.

The existing statutory authority specifically directs the Secretary to issue regulations establishing risk-based performance standards for the security of chemical facilities.[6] These regulations are to apply only to chemical facilities that the Secretary determines present high levels of security risk. The regulations are to require vulnerability assessments and the development and implementation of site security plans from these high-risk chemical facilities.

The vulnerability assessment and site security plan requirements of Subsection 2101(a) of the new title would likely affect more chemical facilities than the existing statutory requirements. Under the current CFATS regulation, DHS does not require all chemical facilities with greater than screening threshold quantities of chemicals of interest to submit vulnerability assessments and site security plans. Only those facilities identified by DHS as high-risk must submit vulnerability assessments and site security plans. Approximately 36,000 facilities have reported possessing a chemical of interest above a screening threshold quantity, while DHS regulates approximately 4,000 of these facilities as high risk.[7] The Subsection 2101(a) requirement that a chemical facility of interest must submit a vulnerability assessment and site security plan may lead to DHS receiving such documents from the approximately 36,000 facilities.

Layered Security in Site Security Plans

Subsection 2101(b) of the new title would, like the existing statutory authority,[8] allow a facility to use layered security measures in its site security plan to address the security vulnerability assessment and the risk-based performance standards.

Approval and Disapproval of Site Security Plans

Subsection 2101(c) of the new title contains four provisions regarding approval and disapproval of site security plans. The first would, like the existing statute,[9] require the Secretary to review and approve each security vulnerability assessment and site security plan and prohibit the Secretary from requiring the presence or absence of a particular security measure to obtain approval. The Secretary would be allowed to disapprove a site security plan that fails to satisfy the risk-based performance standards.

The second provision would allow the Secretary to approve alternative private or governmental security programs that meet the Secretary's requirements. This provision would also explicitly allow a covered chemical facility to meet the site security plan requirement by adopting an alternative security program reviewed and approved by the Secretary. The existing statute permits the Secretary to approve an alternative security program,[10] but does not provide explicit approval for a facility to use such a program to meet the site security plan requirement. The current CFATS regulation allows all regulated entities to meet the site security planning requirement through

---

[6] Subsection 2107(a) of the new title that would be created by Subsection 2(a) of H.R. 4007, as passed the House, would authorize the Secretary to promulgate regulations to implement the new title.

[7] For more information about implementation of the CFATS regulations, see CRS Report R43346, *Implementation of Chemical Facility Anti-Terrorism Standards (CFATS): Issues for Congress*, by Dana A. Shea.

[8] P.L. 109-295, Section 550(a).

[9] P.L. 109-295, Section 550(a).

[10] P.L. 109-295, Section 550(a).

submission of an alternative security program.[11] Consequently, some analysts may view this language as making the current regulatory approach explicit in statute.

The third provision would require the Secretary to employ risk assessment policies and procedures developed under the new title when approving or disapproving a site security plan. However, it would prohibit the Secretary from requiring resubmission of site security information from a covered chemical facility that had received approval prior to the enactment of the new title, if the sole reason for resubmission was that enactment.

The fourth provision would allow DHS to consult with GAO regarding the applicability of a third-party accreditation program. This provision is not present in the current statute.

Audits and Inspections, Noncompliance, Personnel Surety, Facility Access, and Information Availability

Subsection 2101(d) of the new title addresses compliance and contains five provisions. The first provision addresses audits and inspections. Like the existing statute,[12] it requires the Secretary to audit and inspect covered chemical facilities. It differs from the existing statute in that it would expressly allow the Secretary to use non-DHS and nongovernmental inspectors in the inspection process. This subsection would also establish a reporting structure and certain standards and requirements for non-DHS and nongovernmental personnel who conduct such audits or inspections. In addition, it would require the Secretary to prescribe certain standards for training and retraining of auditors and inspectors employed by DHS.

In 2007, during comment on the CFATS interim final rule, some stakeholders expressed concerns about DHS use of third-party inspectors. As described by DHS, these concerns included:

- potential conflicts of interest among third-party inspectors and members of the regulated community;

- potential disclosure of facility business and security information;

- potential inconsistency in training and inspection standards between federal and third-party inspectors; and

- the need for DHS to establish necessary qualifications, certification, and indemnification for third-party inspectors.

Also, some stakeholders asserted that DHS might increase the rate of site security plan approvals through the use of third-party inspectors.[13] The DHS itself raised questions about the appropriateness of DHS use of third-party auditors and if so, what their standards and requirements would be.[14] The express authorization for DHS to use and set standards for non-DHS and nongovernmental inspectors as included in Subsection 2101(d) would likely resolve DHS questions regarding appropriateness of use and establishment of standards.

---

[11] The DHS refers to such programs interchangeably as "alternate" and "alternative" (6 CFR 27.235(a)).

[12] P.L. 109-295, Section 550(e).

[13] 72 *Federal Register* 17688-17745 (April 9, 2007) at 17711.

[14] 72 *Federal Register* 17688–17745 (April 9, 2007) at 17712.

The second provision in Subsection 2101(d) addresses noncompliance by a covered chemical facility. Like the existing statute,[15] it would require the Secretary, upon discovering noncompliance, to provide the owner or operator of the facility with written notification, including an explanation of any deficiency; provide opportunity for consultation; and issue an order to comply by a specified date. If noncompliance continues, the Secretary would be allowed to issue an order for the facility to cease operation. Unlike the existing statute, this provision would require that written notification must occur no later than 14 days after a determination of noncompliance; would direct that consultation following a written notification of a facility be with "the Secretary or the Secretary's designee"; and would allow the Secretary to issue an order to cease operation only if noncompliance exists "after the date specified" in such an order to comply. The existing statute only requires written notification and identification of an opportunity for unspecified consultation. It does not expressly limit the Secretary's ability to issue an order to cease operation. It instead states that such an order may be issued in the case of an owner or operator continuing to be noncompliant.[16]

The third provision, which has no comparable provision in the existing statute, addresses personnel surety. It would direct the Secretary to establish a personnel surety program that would require submission of information only once, provide participating facilities with feedback about individuals submitted for vetting, and provide redress to individuals who believe the submitted information was inaccurate. It would allow a covered chemical facility to use any federal screening program that periodically vets individuals against the terrorist screening database to satisfy its obligation under a personnel surety performance standard. It would prohibit the Secretary from requiring a covered chemical facility to submit any information about an individual unless the individual is vetted under the DHS personnel surety program (in contrast to another federal screening program) or has been identified by the Secretary as presenting a terrorism security risk. Finally, it would require the DHS Security Screening Coordination Office to expedite the development of a common credential and would require DHS to report annually on progress toward this requirement.

The use of other federal screening programs to meet a CFATS personnel surety requirement has been an issue of contention. The DHS has issued an information collection request proposing a personnel surety program.[17] The personnel surety proposal issued by DHS would accept credentials that are vetted recurrently against the terrorist screening database and have their validity verified on a continuing basis by electronic or other means.[18] The DHS has stated that it would not accept, in lieu of its own program, other personnel surety programs that vet individuals on a different schedule.[19] This position would appear to conflict with the requirements in Subsection 2101(d).

---

[15] P.L. 109-295, Section 550(g).

[16] P.L. 109-295, Section 550(g).

[17] 78 *Federal Register* 17680-17701 (March 22, 2013).

[18] According to DHS, the Transportation Worker Identification Credential (TWIC) Program, Hazardous Materials Endorsement (HME) Program, as well as the NEXUS, Secure Electronic Network for Travelers Rapid Inspection (SENTRI), Free and Secure Trade (FAST), and Global Entry Trusted Traveler Programs conduct recurrent vetting (78 *Federal Register* 17680-17701 [March 22, 2013] at 17681-17682).

[19] David Wulf, Director, Infrastructure Security Compliance Division, National Protection and Programs Directorate, Department of Homeland Security, *Letter to Cynthia Hilton, Executive Vice President, Institute of Makers of Explosives*, March 11, 2013.

The fourth provision of the subsection addresses facility access. It would generally prohibit the Secretary from requiring a facility to submit any information about an individual who has been granted facility access. The DHS may require information submission only if DHS has vetted the individual under its personnel surety program or identified the individual as presenting a terrorism security risk. The DHS, under its proposed personnel surety program information collection request, would require facilities to submit information on personnel with access to the regulated areas of a facility. This submission would generally be regardless of credential possession, unless the facility installs electronic readers able to query an approved credential. Facilities would submit different information for individuals with recurrently vetted credentials than for other individuals. This provision would appear to prohibit a requirement to submit this information to DHS to obtain access to a facility.

The fifth provision is not present in the current statutory authority. This provision would require the Secretary to share with the owner or operator of a covered chemical facility such information as the owner or operator needs to comply with Section 2101. The provision may raise questions such as whether the Secretary or the owner or operator determines what information is needed, how such information should be protected, and how such information should be requested and provided. This provision also affirmatively requires the Secretary to share information with owners or operators. A later provision that addresses information sharing with states and local government does not make such an affirmative requirement, but rather permits the Secretary to share as the Secretary deems appropriate.[20]

Responsibilities of the Secretary

Subsection 2101(e) of the new title identifies certain responsibilities of the Secretary and contains three provisions: one on identifying chemical facilities of interest, one on risk assessment, and one on changes in facility tiering. None of these provisions are present in the existing statutory authority.

The first provision would require the Secretary to consult with the heads of other federal agencies, states and political subdivisions thereof, and relevant business associations to identify all chemical facilities of interest.

The second would require the Secretary to develop a risk assessment approach and corresponding tiering methodology incorporating all relevant elements of risk, including threat, vulnerability, and consequence. It would further require that the criteria for determining a facility's security risk include the relevant threat information, the potential economic consequences of a terrorism incident at the facility and the potential loss of human life, and the vulnerability of the facility to certain terrorist events.

The third would require the Secretary to maintain records that reflect the basis for any determination that a facility is no longer subject to the regulatory requirements due to a change in risk tier. In addition to the basis for the determination, the records would include how that basis was confirmed by the Secretary.

---

[20] Subsection 2102(b) of the new title.

Definitions

Subsection 2101(f) of the new title would define certain terms. It would define a "covered chemical facility" as a chemical facility of interest that the Secretary determines meets certain security risk criteria. This subsection would exempt from the definition of "covered chemical facility" those facilities regulated under the Maritime Transportation Security Act of 2002 (MTSA), public water systems as defined by Section 1401 of the Safe Drinking Water Act, wastewater treatment works as defined in Section 212 of the Federal Water Pollution Control Act, any facility owned or operated by the Department of Defense or the Department of Energy, and any facility subject to regulation by the Nuclear Regulatory Commission.[21] The existing statute exempts facilities of these types from all regulation under the statute.

It would define a "chemical facility of interest" as a facility that holds certain chemicals above a certain quantity determined by the Secretary. No types of facility are exempt from the definition of "chemical facility of interest." The existing statute does not contain a similar definition.

The presence of exemptions to the definition of "covered chemical facility" but not to the definition of "chemical facility of interest" may have certain impacts. Facilities of the types exempt from the definition of covered chemical facility may have to meet requirements applying to both chemical facilities of interest and covered chemical facilities, such as those found in Subsection 2101(a) of the new title. Requirements established for chemical facilities of interest may apply to those facilities even though they are exempt from further requirements applying to covered chemical facilities.

Section 2102, Protection and Sharing of Information

Section 2102 of the new title has four provisions addressing protection and sharing of information. Three are similar to existing statutory authority.[22] Subsection 2102(a) of the new title would protect information developed pursuant to the act from disclosure in a manner consistent with that established under MTSA. Subsection 2102(b) of the new title would allow for the sharing of information with state and local government officials, including law enforcement officials and first responders, who possess the necessary security clearances. Subsection 2102(d) of the new title would direct that in any enforcement proceeding, information submitted to or obtained by the Secretary shall be treated as if the information were classified material. These provisions in the existing statutory authority form the basis for DHS's designation of Chemical-terrorism Vulnerability Information (CVI).[23] While Subsection 2102(a) and Subsection 2102(b) reference "information developed pursuant to this title," Subsection 2102(d) of the new title refers to proceedings and information "under this section." This reference, rather than "under this title," may limit the applicability and effectiveness of Subsection 2102(d), since Section 2102 addresses information sharing rather than the program as a whole. The equivalent language in P.L. 109-295, Section 550, also states "under this section," but it applies to the entire existing statutory authority, since that is fully contained in Section 550.[24]

---

[21] P.L. 109-295, Section 550(a).

[22] P.L. 109-295, Section 550(c).

[23] 72 *Federal Register* 17688–17745 (April 9, 2007) at 17715.

[24] For legal analysis of this legislation, please contact the American Law Division of CRS.

Subsection 2102(c) of the new title is not present in the existing statutory authority. It would require the Secretary to provide such information as is necessary to help ensure that first responders are prepared and provided with the situational awareness they need to respond to incidents at covered chemical facilities. It would require this information to be provided to state, local, and regional fusion centers and disseminated through the Homeland Security Information Network or the Homeland Security Data Network, as appropriate.

Section 2103, Civil Penalties

Section 2103 of the new title contains two provisions on civil penalties, both of which are in the existing statutory authority.[25] As under the existing statute, Subsection 2103(a) of the new title would establish a civil penalty of not more than $25,000 per day of violation. Also as under the existing statute, Subsection 2103(b) of the new title would deny any person except the Secretary a right of action to enforce any provision of the new title against an owner or operator of a covered chemical facility.

Section 2104. Whistleblower Protections

Section 2104 of the new title would require the Secretary to publish on the DHS website, and in other publicly available materials, the protections that attach to an individual who provides DHS with "whistleblower" information about covered chemical facilities. The current statutory authority contains no comparable provision.

Section 2105, Relationship to Other Laws

Section 2105 of the new title contains three provisions addressing the relationship of the new title to other laws. Two of the provisions are present in the current statutory authority.[26] Subsection 2105(a) of the new title would affirm that nothing in that title shall be construed to supersede, amend, alter, or affect any federal law that regulates the manufacture, distribution in commerce, use, sale, other treatment, or disposal of chemical substances or mixtures. Subsection 2105(b) of the new title would affirm that it would not preclude a state or political subdivision of a state from establishing more stringent requirements for covered chemical facilities unless an actual conflict exists. As in Section 2102 of the new title, this latter provision refers to standards "issued under this section" and "actual conflict between this Section and the law of that State" rather than referencing the new title as a whole.[27]

The third provision, Subsection 2105(c) of the new title, would require the Secretary to coordinate with the Assistant Secretary of Homeland Security (Transportation Security Administration) to "eliminate any provision of this title applicable to rail security" that would duplicate a security measure under 49 C.F.R. 1580. It also would clarify that in the case of a conflict between regulations established under the new title and those under the jurisdiction of TSA, the TSA regulation prevails. In addition, it would exempt rail transit facilities and rail facilities[28] regulated under Subpart 3 of 49 C.F.R. 1580 (this likely refers to Subpart B of 49

---

[25] P.L. 109-295, Section 550(d).

[26] P.L. 109-295, Section 550(f) and Section 550(h).

[27] For legal analysis of this legislation, please contact the American Law Division of CRS.

[28] In general, "rail facilities" references locations handling rail cargo, while "rail transit facilities" references locations (continued...)

C.F.R. 1580, which addresses rail cargo transportation security) from any requirement to submit Top-Screen information.[29] This would create another statutory exemption from CFATS regulation. Currently, DHS does not require railroad facilities to submit Top-Screen information in order for DHS to determine their security risk under CFATS.[30] Consequently, some analysts may view this language as making the current regulatory approach explicit in statute.

Section 2106, Reports

Section 2106 of the new title contains two provisions that would create reporting requirements. These reporting requirements are not present in the current statutory authority. Subsection 2106(a) of the new title would require the Secretary to submit to Congress, no later than 18 months after enactment, a report on the CFATS program. The report would include a certification by the Secretary of significant progress in identifying all chemical facilities of interest, a description of the steps taken to achieve such progress, and the metrics used to measure it. The report would also include a certification by the Secretary that he or she has developed a risk assessment approach and corresponding tiering methodology as directed by Section 2101 of the new title. Finally, the report would require the Secretary to assess the implementation of any recommendations made by the Homeland Security Studies and Analysis Institute as outlined in the Institute's "Tiering Methodology Peer Review" (Publication Number: RP12-22-02). Subsection 2106(b) of the new title would require the Comptroller General (i.e., the Government Accountability Office) to submit a report to Congress every six months assessing the act's implementation, starting 180 days after the date of enactment. This reporting requirement would expire three years after enactment.

Section 2107, CFATS Regulations

Section 2107 of the new title addresses the issuance and use of regulations to implement the new title and contains four provisions. Subsection 2107(a) would authorize the Secretary to promulgate regulations. Subsection 2107(b) would authorize the Secretary to promulgate or amend any CFATS regulation already in effect to carry out the requirements of the new title. Subsection 2107(c) would define "CFATS regulations" as guidance published or regulations promulgated under the existing authority granted by Section 550 of P.L. 109-295. Subsection 2107(d) would require the Secretary to rely exclusively on the authority provided in the new title for identifying chemicals of interest, designating chemicals of interest, and determining a chemical facility's security risk. The existing statute states that regulations issued under Section 550 of P.L. 109-295 shall apply until expressly superseded.[31]

(...continued)

handling passenger rail.

[29] The Top-Screen is the initial screening process through which chemical facilities provide information to DHS under CFATS.

[30] See http://www.dhs.gov/identifying-facilities-covered-chemical-security-regulation and 72 *Federal Register* 17688-17745 (April 9, 2007) at 17699.

[31] P.L. 109-295, Section 550(b).

Section 2108, Small Covered Chemical Facilities

Section 2108 of the new title would allow the Secretary to provide guidance and tools to small covered chemical facilities to assist in developing their physical security. It would define a small covered chemical facility as a covered chemical facility that employs fewer than 350 employees at the covered chemical facility, and is not a branch or subsidiary of another entity. The Secretary would be required to submit a report to Congress on best practices that may assist small chemical facilities in developing physical security best practices. This report would be delivered to the House Committee on Homeland Security and the Senate Committee on Homeland Security and Governmental Affairs. The existing statute contains no comparable provision.

Section 2109, Outreach to Chemical Facilities of Interest

Section 2109 of the new title addresses outreach to chemical facilities of interest. It would require the Secretary to coordinate with relevant business associations and federal and state agencies to establish an outreach implementation plan within 90 days of enactment. This implementation plan would be to identify chemical facilities of interest and make available compliance assistance materials and information on education and training. The existing statute contains no comparable provision.

Section 2110, Authorization of Appropriations

Section 2110 of the new title would authorize appropriations to carry out the new title for FY2015 through FY2017 at the level of $81 million per year.[32] The existing statute contains no express authorization of appropriations. For FY2015, the Administration requested $87.436 million for the Infrastructure Security Compliance Division, which implements CFATS. For FY2014, the 113th Congress provided $81 million.

Other Provisions of Section 2, Chemical Facility Anti-Terrorism Standards Program

Subsection 2(b) of H.R. 4007, as passed by the House, would amend the table of contents of the Homeland Security Act to reflect the addition of the new title.

Subsection 2(c) of H.R. 4007, as passed by the House, would require the Secretary to commission a third-party study to assess vulnerabilities to acts of terrorism associated with the current CFATS program authorized under P.L. 109-295, Section 550.

Subsection 2(d) of H.R. 4007, as passed by the House, would require the Secretary to submit a plan for using metrics to assess CFATS program effectiveness. This plan would include benchmarks for DHS use of the metrics and information on how DHS plans to use such information for program analysis. The plan would be due 180 days after enactment.

---

[32] H.R. 4007, as reported, would have provided $87.436 million per year for FY2015 through FY2017. See H.Rept. 113-491, p. 6.

Section 3, Effective Date

Section 3 of H.R. 4007, as passed by the House, would establish that the act would take effect 30 days after enactment.

Issues Raised by the Administration

Executive branch agencies have raised several issues with regard to chemical facility security in testimony or in official reports. H.R. 4007, as passed the House, addresses some of these issues directly. This section does not attempt to discuss these issues in the broader policy context, but instead compares them with action taken in the context of H.R. 4007, as passed by the House. For more information on these issues, including discussion of various policy alternatives, see CRS Report R42918, *Chemical Facility Security: Issues and Options for the 113th Congress*, by Dana A. Shea.

Inclusion of Inherently Safer Technologies

Previous debate on chemical facility security has included whether to mandate the adoption or consideration of changes in chemical processes to reduce the potential consequences following a successful attack on a chemical facility. Suggestions for such changes have included reducing the amount of chemical stored onsite and changing the chemicals used. In previous congressional debate, these approaches have been referred to as inherently safer technologies or methods to reduce the consequences of a terrorist attack.

In 2010, the Obama Administration expressed its position on the use of inherently safer technologies to enhance security at high-risk chemical facilities in some circumstances. It established a series of principles directing its policy:

> The Administration supports consistency of inherently safer technology approaches for facilities regardless of sector.
>
> The Administration believes that all high-risk chemical facilities, Tiers 1-4, should assess [inherently safer technology] methods and report the assessment in the facilities' site security plans. Further, the appropriate regulatory entity should have the authority to require facilities posing the highest degree of risk (Tiers 1 and 2) to implement inherently safer technology methods if such methods demonstrably enhance overall security, are determined to be feasible, and, in the case of water sector facilities, consider public health and environmental requirements.
>
> The Administration believes that the appropriate regulatory entity should review the inherently safer technology assessment contained in the site security plan for all Tier 3 and Tier 4 facilities. The entity should be authorized to provide recommendations on implementing inherently safer technologies, but it would not have the authority to require facilities to implement the inherently safer technology methods.

> The Administration believes that flexibility and staggered implementation would be required in implementing this new inherently safer technology policy.[33]

H.R. 4007, as passed by the House, maintains the existing statutory language that prohibits the Secretary from disapproving a site security plan based on the presence or absence of a particular security measure. The DHS has interpreted this statutory language as prohibiting it from requiring consideration or implementation of inherently safer technologies.

Long-Term Authorization

While the Obama Administration FY2015 budget request seeks an extension of the statutory authority until October 4, 2015, the Obama Administration has also supported enacting a longer or permanent statutory authority.[34] In response to Executive Order 13650, *Improving Chemical Facility Safety and Security*,[35] the Administration established a multi-agency Chemical Facility Safety and Security Working Group co-chaired by the Department of Homeland Security, Environmental Protection Agency, and Department of Labor. In May 2014, the working group issued a report to the President that called for congressional action to provide permanent statutory authorization for the CFATS program.[36] H.R. 4007, as passed by the House, lacks a statutory termination date and would provide a permanent statutory authorization. It also provides a three-year authorization of appropriations through FY2017.

CFATS Enforcement Process

The report of the Chemical Facility Safety and Security Working Group established in response to Executive Order 13650 also called for congressional action to change the CFATS enforcement process.[37] The report notes that the current statute requires a multi-step enforcement process before DHS can fine or shut down a facility for noncompliance. It asserts that the ability to immediately issue orders to assess civil penalties or to close down a facility for violations, without having to first issue an order calling for correction of the violation, is an important ability that DHS lacks. The report states, "Congress should provide this streamlined enforcement authority so that, in circumstances in which a facility's noncompliance presents an immediate threat, DHS can act quickly to safeguard the facility and protect the public from potential acts of terrorism."[38] H.R. 4007, as passed by the House, would retain the existing statute's general

---

[33] Testimony of Rand Beers, Under Secretary, National Protection and Programs Directorate, Department of Homeland Security, before the Senate Committee on Homeland Security and Governmental Affairs, March 3, 2010. See also Personal Communication between CRS and Office of Legislative Affairs, Department of Homeland Security, January 16, 2014.

[34] Oral testimony of Rand Beers, Under Secretary, National Protection and Programs Directorate, Department of Homeland Security, before the House Committee on Homeland Security, Subcommittee on Cybersecurity, Infrastructure Protection, and Security Technologies, February 11, 2011.

[35] 78 *Federal Register* 48029-48032 (August 7, 2013).

[36] Chemical Facility Safety and Security Working Group, *Executive Order 13650: Actions to Improve Chemical Facility Safety and Security-A Shared Commitment*, Report to the President, May 2014, p. 46, https://www.osha.gov/chemicalexecutiveorder/final_chemical_eo_status_report.pdf.

[37] Chemical Facility Safety and Security Working Group, *Executive Order 13650: Actions to Improve Chemical Facility Safety and Security-A Shared Commitment*, Report to the President, May 2014, p. 46, https://www.osha.gov/chemicalexecutiveorder/final_chemical_eo_status_report.pdf.

[38] Chemical Facility Safety and Security Working Group, *Executive Order 13650: Actions to Improve Chemical Facility Safety and Security-A Shared Commitment*, Report to the President, May 2014, p. 46, https://www.osha.gov/ (continued...)

---

enforcement structure, which requires that the Secretary provide the facility owner or operator with written notification, an opportunity for consultation, and issue an order to comply by a specific date before issuing an order for civil penalty or to cease operation.

Removal of Water and Wastewater Exemptions

Since 2008, DHS and the Environmental Protection Agency (EPA) have called for additional authorities to regulate water and wastewater treatment facilities:

> The Department of Homeland Security and the Environmental Protection Agency believe that there is an important gap in the framework for regulating the security of chemicals at water and wastewater treatment facilities in the United States. The authority for regulating the chemical industry purposefully excludes from its coverage water and wastewater treatment facilities. We need to work with the Congress to close this gap in the chemical security authorities in order to secure chemicals of interest at these facilities and protect the communities they serve. Water and wastewater treatment facilities that are determined to be high-risk due to the presence of chemicals of interest should be regulated for security in a manner that is consistent with the CFATS risk and performance-based framework while also recognizing the unique public health and environmental requirements and responsibilities of such facilities.[39]

In 2010, EPA testified that the Obama Administration believes that EPA should be the lead agency for chemical security for both drinking water and wastewater systems, with DHS supporting EPA's efforts.[40]

In contrast, the May 2014 report to the President by the Chemical Facility Safety and Security Working Group called for action from Congress to remove the exemption for water and wastewater treatment facilities. According to the report, DHS could then regulate security at these facilities in collaboration with the EPA.[41]

H.R. 4007, as passed by the House, would exempt water and wastewater treatment facilities from the definition of covered chemical facility. According to the House report accompanying H.R. 4007, as passed the House:

> The Committee did not alter these exemptions from Sec. 550. First required by Congress to do vulnerability assessments and emergency response plans in 2002 under the Public Health Security and Bioterrorism Preparedness and Response Act (Safe Drinking Water Act Sections 1433–1435), drinking water facilities are covered under a mature regulatory scheme

---

(...continued)

chemicalexecutiveorder/final_chemical_eo_status_report.pdf.

[39] Testimony of Benjamin H. Grumbles, Assistant Administrator for Water, U.S. Environmental Protection Agency before the House Committee on Energy and Commerce, Subcommittee on Environment and Hazardous Materials, June 12, 2008. See also testimony of Rand Beers, Under Secretary, National Protection and Programs Directorate, Department of Homeland Security, before the Senate Committee on Homeland Security and Governmental Affairs, March 3, 2010.

[40] Testimony of Peter S. Silva, Assistant Administrator for Water, Environmental Protection Agency, before the Senate Committee on Homeland Security and Governmental Affairs, March 3, 2010.

[41] Chemical Facility Safety and Security Working Group, *Executive Order 13650: Actions to Improve Chemical Facility Safety and Security-A Shared Commitment*, Report to the President, May 2014, pp. 46-47, https://www.osha.gov/chemicalexecutiveorder/final_chemical_eo_status_report.pdf.

that is working well. Moreover, according to the DHS Inspector General, the United States contains approximately 52,000 community water systems and 16,500 wastewater treatment facilities. Thus, although some have called for a removal of these exemptions, the Committee believes that to expand the CFATS mission to cover an additional 70,000 facilities—at precisely the time when the program is working to successfully manage its basic responsibilities—would be misguided.[42]

Therefore, DHS would not have authority to regulate public water systems, as defined by Section 1401 of the Safe Drinking Water Act, and wastewater treatment works, as defined in Section 212 of the Federal Water Pollution Control Act, as covered chemical facilities.

---

[42] H.Rept. 113-491, p. 22.

Appendix. Side-by-Side Comparison of H.R. 4007, as Passed by the House, and P.L. 109-295, Section 550, as Amended

Table A-1. Side-by-Side Comparison of H.R. 4007, as Passed by the House, and P.L. 109-295, Section 550, as Amended

H.R. 4007, as Passed by the House	P.L. 109-295, Section 550, as Amended
SECTION 1. SHORT TITLE.	No comparable provision
This Act may be cited as the "Chemical Facility Anti-Terrorism Standards Program Authorization and Accountability Act of 2014".	
SEC. 2. CHEMICAL FACILITY ANTI-TERRORISM STANDARDS PROGRAM.	No comparable provision
(a) IN GENERAL.—The Homeland Security Act of 2002 (6 U.S.C. 101 et seq.) is amended by adding at the end the following:	
"TITLE XXI—CHEMICAL FACILITY ANTI–TERRORISM STANDARDS	
"SEC. 2101. CHEMICAL FACILITY ANTI-TERRORISM STANDARDS PROGRAM.	
"(a) PROGRAM ESTABLISHED.—There is in the Department a Chemical Facility Anti-Terrorism Standards Program.	SEC. 550(a) No later than six months after the date of enactment of this Act,
Under such Program, the Secretary shall establish risk-based performance standards designed to protect covered chemical facilities and chemical facilities of interest from acts of terrorism and other security risks and	the Secretary of Homeland Security shall issue interim final regulations establishing risk-based performance standards for security of chemical facilities and [SEC. 550(a)]
require such facilities to submit security vulnerability assessments and	requiring vulnerability assessments and [SEC. 550(a)]
to develop and implement site security plans.	the development and implementation of site security plans for chemical facilities: [SEC. 550(a)]
"(b) SECURITY MEASURES.—Site security plans required under subsection (a) may include layered security measures that, in combination, appropriately address the security vulnerability assessment and the risk-based performance standards for security for the facility.	Provided further, That such regulations shall permit each such facility, in developing and implementing site security plans, to select layered security measures that, in combination, appropriately address the vulnerability assessment and the risk-based performance standards for security for the facility: [SEC. 550(a)]
"(c) APPROVAL OR DISAPPROVAL OF SITE SECURITY PLANS.—	
"(1) IN GENERAL.—The Secretary shall review and approve or disapprove each security vulnerability assessment and site security plan under subsection (a).	Provided further, That the Secretary shall review and approve each vulnerability assessment and site security plan required under this section: [SEC. 550(a)]

H.R. 4007, as Passed by the House	P.L. 109-295, Section 550, as Amended
The Secretary may not disapprove a site security plan based on the presence or absence of a particular security measure, but the Secretary shall disapprove a site security plan if the plan fails to satisfy the risk-based performance standards established under subsection (a).	Provided further, That the Secretary may not disapprove a site security plan submitted under this section based on the presence or absence of a particular security measure, but the Secretary may disapprove a site security plan if the plan fails to satisfy the risk-based performance standards established by this section: [SEC. 550(a)]
"(2) ALTERNATIVE SECURITY PROGRAMS.—The Secretary may approve an alternative security program established by a private sector entity or a Federal, State, or local authority or pursuant to other applicable laws, if the Secretary determines that the requirements of such program meet the requirements of this section.	Provided further, That the Secretary may approve alternative security programs established by private sector entities, Federal, State, or local authorities, or other applicable laws if the Secretary determines that the requirements of such programs meet the requirements of this section and the interim regulations: [SEC. 550(a)]
A covered chemical facility may meet the site security plan requirement under subsection (a) by adopting an alternative security program that has been reviewed and approved by the Secretary under this paragraph.	No comparable provision
"(3) SITE SECURITY PLAN ASSESSMENTS.—In approving or disapproving a site security plan under this subsection, the Secretary shall employ the risk assessment policies and procedures developed under this title. In the case of a covered chemical facility for which a site security plan has been approved by the Secretary before the date of the enactment of this title, the Secretary may not require the resubmission of the site security information solely by reason of the enactment of this title.	No comparable provision
"(4) CONSULTATION.—The Secretary may consult with the Government Accountability Office to investigate the feasibility and applicability a third party accreditation program that would work with industry stakeholders to develop site security plans that may be applicable to all similarly situated facilities. The program would include the development of Program-Specific Handbooks for facilities to reference on site.	No comparable provision
"(d) COMPLIANCE.—	
"(1) AUDITS AND INSPECTIONS.—	
"(A) IN GENERAL.—The Secretary shall conduct the audit and inspection of covered chemical facilities for the purpose of determining compliance with this Act.	SEC. 550(e) The Secretary of Homeland Security shall audit and inspect chemical facilities for the purposes of determining compliance with the regulations issued pursuant to this section.
The audit and inspection may be carried out by a non-Department or nongovernment entity, as approved by the Secretary.	No comparable provision
"(B) REPORTING STRUCTURE.—Any audit or inspection conducted by an individual employed by a nongovernment entity shall be assigned in coordination with the head of audits and inspections for the region in which the audit or inspection is to be conducted. When in the field, any individual employed by a nongovernment entity shall report to the respective head of audits and inspections for the region in which the individual is operating.	No comparable provision

H.R. 4007, as Passed by the House	P.L. 109-295, Section 550, as Amended
"(C) REQUIREMENTS FOR NONGOVERNMENT PERSONNEL.—If the Secretary arranges for an audit or inspection under subparagraph (A) to be carried out by a nongovernment entity, the Secretary shall require, as a condition of such arrangement, that any individual who conducts the audit or inspection be a citizen of the United States and shall prescribe standards for the qualification of the individuals who carry out such audits and inspections that are commensurate with the standards for a Government auditor or inspector. Such standards shall include—	No comparable provision

"(i) minimum training requirements for new auditors or inspectors;

"(ii) retraining requirements;

"(iii) minimum education and experience levels;

"(iv) the submission of information as required by the Secretary to enable determination of whether the auditor or inspector has a conflict of interest;

"(v) the maintenance of a secret security clearance;

"(vi) reporting any issue of non-compliance with this section to the Secretary within 24 hours; and

"(vii) any additional qualifications for fitness of duty as the Secretary may establish.

| "(D) TRAINING OF DEPARTMENT AUDITORS AND INSPECTORS.—The Secretary shall prescribe standards for the training and retraining of individuals employed by the Department as auditors and inspectors. Such standards shall include— | No comparable provision |

"(i) minimum training requirements for new auditors and inspectors;

"(ii) retraining requirements; and

"(iii) any additional requirements the Secretary may establish.

| "(2) NOTICE OF NONCOMPLIANCE.— | SEC. 550(g) If the Secretary determines that a chemical facility is not in compliance with this section, the Secretary shall provide the owner or operator with [SEC. 550(g)] |
| "(A) NOTICE.—If the Secretary determines that a covered chemical facility or a chemical facility of interest is not in compliance with this section, the Secretary shall— | |

"(i) provide the owner or operator of the facility with—

"(I) written notification (including a clear explanation of any deficiency in the security vulnerability assessment or site security plan) by not later than 14 days after the determination is made; and	written notification (including a clear explanation of deficiencies in the vulnerability assessment and site security plan) and [SEC. 550(g)]
"(II) an opportunity for consultation with the Secretary or the Secretary's designee; and	opportunity for consultation, and [SEC. 550(g)]
"(ii) issue an order to comply by such date as the Secretary determines to be appropriate under the circumstances.	issue an order to comply by such date as the Secretary determines to be appropriate under the circumstances: [SEC. 550(g)]
"(B) CONTINUED NONCOMPLIANCE.—If the owner or operator continues to be in noncompliance after the date specified in such order, the Secretary may enter an order assessing a civil penalty, an order to cease operations, or both.	Provided, That if the owner or operator continues to be in noncompliance, the Secretary may issue an order for the facility to cease operation, until the owner or operator complies with the order. [SEC. 550(g)]

H.R. 4007, as Passed by the House	P.L. 109-295, Section 550, as Amended
"(3) PERSONNEL SURETY.—	No comparable provision
"(A) PERSONNEL SURETY PROGRAM.—For purposes of this title, the Secretary shall carry out a Personnel Surety Program that—	
"(i) does not require an owner or operator of a covered chemical facility that voluntarily participates to submit information about an individual more than one time;	
"(ii) provides a participating owner or operator of a covered chemical facility with feedback about an individual based on vetting the individual against the terrorist screening database, to the extent that such feedback is necessary for the facility's compliance with regulations promulgated under this title; and	
"(iii) provides redress to an individual whose information was vetted against the terrorist screening database under the program and who believes that the personally identifiable information submitted to the Department for such vetting by a covered chemical facility, or its designated representative, was inaccurate.	
"(B) PERSONNEL SURETY IMPLEMENTATION.—To the extent that a risk-based performance standard under subsection (a) is directed toward identifying individuals with terrorist ties—	
"(i) a covered chemical facility may satisfy its obligation under such standard with respect to an individual by utilizing any Federal screening program that periodically vets individuals against the terrorist screening database, or any successor, including the Personnel Surety Program under subparagraph (A); and	
"(ii) the Secretary may not require a covered chemical facility to submit any information about such individual unless the individual—	
"(I) is vetted under the Personnel Surety Program; or	
"(II) has been identified as presenting a terrorism security risk.	
"(C) RESPONSIBILITIES OF SECURITY SCREENING COORDINATION OFFICE.—	
"(i) IN GENERAL.—The Secretary shall direct the Security Screening Coordination Office of the Department to coordinate with the National Protection and Programs Directorate to expedite the development of a common credential that screens against the terrorist screening database on a recurrent basis and meets all other screening requirements of this title.	
"(ii) REPORT.—Not later than March 1, 2015, and annually thereafter, the Secretary shall submit to Congress a report on the progress of the Secretary in meeting the requirements of clause (i).	
"(4) FACILITY ACCESS.—For purposes of the compliance of a covered chemical facility with a risk-based performance standard established under subsection (a), the Secretary may not require the facility to submit any information about an individual who has been granted access to the facility unless the individual—	No comparable provision
"(A) was vetted under the Personnel Surety Program; or	
"(B) has been identified as presenting a terrorism security risk.	

H.R. 4007, as Passed by the House	P.L. 109-295, Section 550, as Amended
"(5) AVAILABILITY OF INFORMATION.—The Secretary shall share with the owner or operator of a covered chemical facility such information as the owner or operator needs to comply with this section.	No comparable provision
"(e) RESPONSIBILITIES OF THE SECRETARY.—	No comparable provision
"(1) IDENTIFICATION OF FACILITIES OF INTEREST.—In carrying out this title, the Secretary shall consult with the heads of other Federal agencies, States and political subdivisions thereof, and relevant business associations to identify all chemical facilities of interest.	
"(2) RISK ASSESSMENT.—	No comparable provision
"(A) IN GENERAL.—For purposes of this title, the Secretary shall develop a risk assessment approach and corresponding tiering methodology that incorporates all relevant elements of risk, including threat, vulnerability, and consequence.	
"(B) CRITERIA FOR DETERMINING SECURITY RISK.—The criteria for determining the security risk of terrorism associated with a facility shall include—	
"(i) the relevant threat information;	
"(ii) the potential economic consequences and the potential loss of human life in the event of the facility being subject to a terrorist attack, compromise, infiltration, or exploitation; and	
"(iii) the vulnerability of the facility to a terrorist attack, compromise, infiltration, or exploitation.	
"(3) CHANGES IN TIERING.—Any time that tiering for a covered chemical facility is changed and the facility is determined to no longer be subject to the requirements of this title, the Secretary shall maintain records to reflect the basis for this determination. The records shall include information on whether and how the information that was the basis for the determination was confirmed by the Secretary.	No comparable provision
"(f) DEFINITIONS.—In this title:	
"(1) The term 'covered chemical facility' means a facility that the Secretary identifies as a chemical facility of interest and, based upon review of a Top-Screen, as such term is defined in section 27.105 of title 6 of Code of Federal Regulations, determines meets the risk criteria developed pursuant subsection (e)(2)(B).	Provided, That such regulations shall apply to chemical facilities that, in the discretion of the Secretary, present high levels of security risk: [SEC. 550(a)]
Such term does not include any of the following:	Provided further, That the Secretary shall not apply regulations issued pursuant to this section to facilities regulated pursuant to the Maritime Transportation Security Act of 2002, Public Law 107–295, as amended; [SEC. 550(a)]
"(A) A facility regulated pursuant to the Maritime Transportation Security Act of 2002 (Public Law 107–295).	
"(B) A Public Water System, as such term is defined by section 1401 of the Safe Drinking Water Act (Public Law 93–523; 42 U.S.C. 300f).	Public Water Systems, as defined by section 1401 of the Safe Drinking Water Act, Public Law 93– 523, as amended; [SEC. 550(a)]
"(C) A Treatment Works, as such term is defined in section 212 of the Federal Water Pollution Control Act (Public Law 92–500; 33 U.S.C. 12920).	Treatment Works as defined in section 212 of the Federal Water Pollution Control Act, Public Law 92–500, as amended; [SEC. 550(a)]

H.R. 4007, as Passed by the House	P.L. 109-295, Section 550, as Amended
"(D) Any facility owned or operated by the Department of Defense or the Department of Energy.	any facility owned or operated by the Department of Defense or the Department of Energy, or [SEC. 550(a)]
"(E) Any facility subject to regulation by the Nuclear Regulatory Commission.	any facility subject to regulation by the Nuclear Regulatory Commission. [SEC. 550(a)]
"(2) The term 'chemical facility of interest' means a facility that holds, or that the Secretary has a reasonable basis to believe holds, a Chemical of Interest, as designated under in Appendix A of title 6 of the Code of Federal Regulations, at a threshold quantity that meets relevant risk-related criteria developed pursuant to subsection (e)(2)(B).[a]	No comparable provision

"SEC. 2102. PROTECTION AND SHARING OF INFORMATION.

H.R. 4007, as Passed by the House	P.L. 109-295, Section 550, as Amended
"(a) IN GENERAL.—Notwithstanding any other provision of law, information developed pursuant to this title, including vulnerability assessments, site security plans, and other security related information, records, and documents shall be given protections from public disclosure consistent with similar information developed by chemical facilities subject to regulation under section 70103 of title 46, United States Code.	SEC. 550(c) Notwithstanding any other provision of law and subsection (b), information developed under this section, including vulnerability assessments, site security plans, and other security related information, records, and documents shall be given protections from public disclosure consistent with similar information developed by chemical facilities subject to regulation under section 70103 of title 46, United States Code: [SEC. 550(c)]
"(b) SHARING OF INFORMATION WITH STATES AND LOCAL GOVERNMENTS.—This section does not prohibit the sharing of information developed pursuant to this title, as the Secretary deems appropriate, with State and local government officials possessing the necessary security clearances, including law enforcement officials and first responders, for the purpose of carrying out this title, if such information may not be disclosed pursuant to any State or local law.	Provided, That this subsection does not prohibit the sharing of such information, as the Secretary deems appropriate, with State and local government officials possessing the necessary security clearances, including law enforcement officials and first responders, for the purpose of carrying out this section, provided that such information may not be disclosed pursuant to any State or local law: [SEC. 550(c)]
"(c) SHARING OF INFORMATION WITH FIRST RESPONDERS.—The Secretary shall provide to State, local, and regional fusion centers (as such term is defined in section 210A(j)(1) of this Act) and State and local government officials, as determined appropriate by the Secretary, such information as is necessary to help ensure that first responders are properly prepared and provided with the situational awareness needed to respond to incidents at covered chemical facilities. Such information shall be disseminated through the Homeland Security Information Network or the Homeland Secure Data Network, as appropriate.	No comparable provision
"(d) ENFORCEMENT PROCEEDINGS.—In any proceeding to enforce this section, vulnerability assessments, site security plans, and other information submitted to or obtained by the Secretary under this section, and related vulnerability or security information, shall be treated as if the information were classified material.	Provided further, That in any proceeding to enforce this section, vulnerability assessments, site security plans, and other information submitted to or obtained by the Secretary under this section, and related vulnerability or security information, shall be treated as if the information were classified material. [SEC. 550(c)]

"SEC. 2103. CIVIL PENALTIES.

H.R. 4007, as Passed by the House	P.L. 109-295, Section 550, as Amended
"(a) VIOLATIONS.—Any person who violates an order issued under this title shall be liable for a civil penalty under section 70119(a) of title 46, United States Code.	SEC. 550(d) Any person who violates an order issued under this section shall be liable for a civil penalty under section 70119(a) of title 46, United States Code:
"(b) RIGHT OF ACTION.—Nothing in this title confers upon any person except the Secretary a right of action against an owner or operator of a covered chemical facility to enforce any provision of this title.	Provided, That nothing in this section confers upon any person except the Secretary a right of action against an owner or operator of a chemical facility to enforce any provision of this section. [SEC. 550(d)]
"SEC. 2104. WHISTLEBLOWER PROTECTIONS.	No comparable provision
"The Secretary shall publish on the Internet website of the Department and in other materials made available to the public the whistleblower protections that an individual providing such information would have.	
"SEC. 2105. RELATIONSHIP TO OTHER LAWS.	
"(a) OTHER FEDERAL LAWS.—Nothing in this title shall be construed to supersede, amend, alter, or affect any Federal law that regulates the manufacture, distribution in commerce, use, sale, other treatment, or disposal of chemical substances or mixtures.	SEC. 550(f) Nothing in this section shall be construed to supersede, amend, alter, or affect any Federal law that regulates the manufacture, distribution in commerce, use, sale, other treatment, or disposal of chemical substances or mixtures.
"(b) STATES AND POLITICAL SUBDIVISIONS.—This title shall not preclude or deny any right of any State or political subdivision thereof to adopt or enforce any regulation, requirement, or standard of performance with respect to chemical facility security that is more stringent than a regulation, requirement, or standard of performance issued under this section, or otherwise impair any right or jurisdiction of any State with respect to chemical facilities within that State, unless there is an actual conflict between this section and the law of that State.	SEC. 550(h) This section shall not preclude or deny any right of any State or political subdivision thereof to adopt or enforce any regulation, requirement, or standard of performance with respect to chemical facility security that is more stringent than a regulation, requirement, or standard of performance issued under this section, or otherwise impair any right or jurisdiction of any State with respect to chemical facilities within that State, unless there is an actual conflict between this section and the law of that State.
"(c) RAIL TRANSIT.—	No comparable provision
"(1) DUPLICATIVE REGULATIONS.—The Secretary shall coordinate with the Assistant Secretary of Homeland Security (Transportation Security Administration) to eliminate any provision of this title applicable to rail security that would duplicate any security measure under the Rail Transportation Security Rule under section 1580 of title 49 of the Code of Federal Regulations, as in effect as of the date of the enactment of this title. To the extent that there is a conflict between this title and any regulation under the jurisdiction of the Transportation Security Administration, the regulation under the jurisdiction of the Transportation Security Administration shall prevail.	
"(2) EXEMPTION FROM TOP-SCREEN.—A rail transit facility or a rail facility, as such terms are defined in section 1580.3 of title 49 of the Code of Federal Regulations, to which subpart 3 of such title applies pursuant to section 1580.100 of such title shall not be required to complete a Top-Screen as such term is defined in section 27.105 of title 6 of the Code of Federal Regulations.[b]	

H.R. 4007, as Passed by the House	P.L. 109-295, Section 550, as Amended
"SEC. 2106. REPORTS.	No comparable provision
"(a) REPORT TO CONGRESS.—Not later than 18 months after the date of the enactment of this title, the Secretary shall submit to Congress a report on the Chemical Facilities Anti-Terrorism Standards Program. Such report shall include each of the following:	
"(1) Certification by the Secretary that the Secretary has made significant progress in the identification of all chemical facilities of interest pursuant to section 2101(e)(1), including a description of the steps taken to achieve such progress and the metrics used to measure it, information on whether facilities that submitted Top-Screens as a result of such efforts were tiered and in what tiers they were placed, and an action plan to better identify chemical facilities of interest and bring those facilities into compliance.	
"(2) Certification by the Secretary that the Secretary has developed a risk assessment approach and corresponding tiering methodology pursuant to section 2101(e)(2).	
"(3) An assessment by the Secretary of the implementation by the Department of any recommendations made by the Homeland Security Studies and Analysis Institute as outlined in the Institute's Tiering Methodology Peer Review (Publication Number: RP12–22–02).	
"(b) SEMIANNUAL GAO REPORT.—During the 3-year period beginning on the date of the enactment of this title, the Comptroller General of the United States shall submit a semiannual report to Congress containing the assessment of the Comptroller General of the implementation of this title. The Comptroller General shall submit the first such report by not later than the date that is 180 days after the date of the enactment of this title.	No comparable provision
"SEC. 2107. CFATS REGULATIONS.	No comparable provision
"(a) IN GENERAL.—The Secretary is authorized, in accordance with chapter 5 of title 5, United States Code, to promulgate regulations implementing the provisions of this title.	
"(b) EXISTING CFATS REGULATIONS.—In carrying out the requirements of this title, the Secretary shall use the CFATS regulations, as in effect immediately before the date of the enactment of this title, that the Secretary determines carry out such requirements, and may issue new regulations or amend such regulations pursuant to the authority in subsection (a).	SEC. 550(b) Interim regulations issued under this section shall apply until the effective date of interim or final regulations promulgated under other laws that establish requirements and standards referred to in subsection (a) and expressly supersede this section:
"(c) DEFINITION OF CFATS REGULATIONS.—In this section, the term 'CFATS regulations' means the regulations prescribed pursuant to section 550 of the Department of Homeland Security Appropriations Act, 2007 (Public Law 109–295; 120 Stat. 1388; 6 U.S.C. 121 note), as well as all Federal Register notices and other published guidance concerning section 550 of the Department of Homeland Security Appropriations Act, 2007.	No comparable provision
"(d) AUTHORITY.—The Secretary shall exclusively rely upon authority provided in this title for determining compliance with this title in—	No comparable provision
"(1) identifying chemicals of interest;	
"(2) designating chemicals of interest; and	
"(3) determining security risk associated with a chemical facility.	

H.R. 4007, as Passed by the House	**P.L. 109-295, Section 550, as Amended**
"SEC. 2108. SMALL COVERED CHEMICAL FACILITIES.	No comparable provision
"(a) IN GENERAL.—The Secretary may provide guidance and, as appropriate, tools, methodologies, or computer software, to assist small covered chemical facilities in developing their physical security.	
"(b) REPORT.—The Secretary shall submit to the Committee on Homeland Security of the House of Representatives and the Committee on Homeland Security and Governmental Affairs of the Senate a report on best practices that may assist small chemical facilities, as defined by the Secretary, in development of physical security best practices.	No comparable provision
"(c) DEFINITION.—For purposes of this section, the term 'small covered chemical facility' means a covered chemical facility that has fewer than 350 employees employed at the covered chemical facility, and is not a branch or subsidiary of another entity.	No comparable provision
"SEC. 2109. OUTREACH TO CHEMICAL FACILITIES OF INTEREST.	No comparable provision
"Not later than 90 days after the date of the enactment of this title, the Secretary shall establish an outreach implementation plan, in coordination with the heads of other appropriate Federal and State agencies and relevant business associations, to identify chemical facilities of interest and make available compliance assistance materials and information on education and training.	
"SEC. 2110. AUTHORIZATION OF APPROPRIATIONS.	No comparable provision
"There is authorized to be appropriated to carry out this title $81,000,000 for each of fiscal years 2015, 2016, and 2017.".	
(b) CLERICAL AMENDMENT.—The table of contents in section 1(b) of such Act is amended by adding at the end the following:	No comparable provision
"TITLE XXI—CHEMICAL FACILITY ANTI–TERRORISM STANDARDS	
"Sec. 2101. Chemical Facility Anti-Terrorism Standards Program.	
"Sec. 2102. Protection and sharing of information.	
"Sec. 2103. Civil penalties.	
"Sec. 2104. Whistleblower protections.	
"Sec. 2105. Relationship to other laws.	
"Sec. 2106. Reports.	
"Sec. 2107. CFATS regulations.	
"Sec. 2108. Small covered chemical facilities.	
"Sec. 2109. Outreach to chemical facilities of interest.	
"Sec. 2110. Authorization of appropriations.".	
(c) THIRD-PARTY ASSESSMENT.—Using amounts authorized to be appropriated under section 2110 of the Homeland Security Act of 2002, as added by subsection (a), the Secretary of Homeland Security shall commission a third-party study to assess vulnerabilities to acts of terrorism associated with the Chemical Facility Anti-Terrorism Standards program, as authorized pursuant to section 550 of the Department of Homeland Security Appropriations Act, 2007 (Public Law 109-295; 120 Stat. 1388; 6 U.S.C. 121 note).	No comparable provision

H.R. 4007, as Passed by the House	P.L. 109-295, Section 550, as Amended
(d) METRICS.—Not later than 180 days after the date of the enactment of this Act, the Secretary shall submit to Congress a plan for the utilization of metrics to assess the effectiveness of the Chemical Facility Anti-Terrorism Standards program to reduce the risk of a terrorist attack or other security risk to those citizens and communities surrounding covered chemical facilities. The plan shall include benchmarks on when the program will begin utilizing the metrics and how the Department of Homeland Security plans to use the information to inform the program.	No comparable provision
SEC. 3. EFFECTIVE DATE.	No comparable provision
This Act, and the amendments made by this Act, shall take effect on the date that is 30 days after the date of the enactment of this Act.	
No comparable provision	Provided, That the authority provided by this section shall terminate on October 4, 2014. [SEC. 550(b)]

Source: CRS analysis of H.R. 4007, as passed the House, and P.L. 109-295, Section 550, as amended.

Notes: The table structure follows the organization of H.R. 4007, as passed the House. Comparable provisions of P.L. 109-295, Section 550, are aligned with those in H.R. 4007, as passed the House.

a. This likely refers to 6 C.F.R. 27 Appendix A, which contains the list of chemicals of interest currently regulated under CFATS.

b. This likely refers to Subpart B of 49 C.F.R. 1580, which addresses rail cargo transportation security.

Author Contact Information

Dana A. Shea
Specialist in Science and Technology Policy
dshea@crs.loc.gov, 7-6844